Our **WILD**™ **WORLD**
SERIES

Manatees

NORTHWORD
Minnetonka, Minnesota

DEDICATION
To my father, retired U.S. Army Chief Warrant Officer Robert F. Feeney, for teaching me how to read.

© NorthWord Press, 2001

Doug Perrine/Innerspace Visions: front cover, back cover, pp. 8-9, 10, 12-13, 14, 17, 20-21, 24, 26-27, 30, 42-43, 44-45; Tom & Therisa Stack/Tom Stack & Associates: pp. 4, 39; Fred Bavendam/Minden Pictures: pp. 5, 29; Fernando Trujillo/Innerspace Visions: p. 7; Brandon D. Cole: pp. 11, 18-19, 22, 36-37, 38, 41; François Gohier: p. 32; Jeff Foott/Tom Stack & Associates: pp. 34-35.

Illustrations by John F. McGee
Designed by Dave W. Schelitzche
Edited by Barbara K. Harold

NorthWord Books for Young Readers
11571 K-Tel Drive
Minnetonka, MN 55343
1-888-255-9989
www.tnkidsbooks.com

Library of Congress Cataloging-in-Publication Data

Feeney, Kathy
    Manatees / Kathy Feeney ; illustrations by John F. Mcgee.
        p. cm. -- (Our wild world series)
    ISBN 1-55971-778-5 (soft cover)
        1. Manatees--Juvenile literature. [1. Manatees.] I. McGee, John F. ill. II. Title. III. Series.
    QL737.S63 F44 2001
    599.55--dc21

                                                                                          00-045563

Printed in Selangor Darul Ehsan Malaysia, June 2013.

Our **WILD**™ **WORLD**
SERIES

Manatees

Kathy Feeney
Illustrations by John F. McGee

NORTHWORD
Minnetonka, Minnesota

MANATEES are often called "gentle giants." The nickname describes the huge size and peaceful personality of these mammals. They are closely related to the elephant but they live in water. Manatees are so mild-mannered that they prefer to just swim away from trouble. They belong to the scientific order, or group, Sirenia. This name means "sea cows" in Greek.

Many people believe manatees were the beginning of a famous legend.

Long ago, sailors reported seeing beautiful creatures resting on rocks, halfway out of the water. As they sailed by on their ships, they heard high-pitched sounds. The sailors thought the noise was made by women singing. When they saw the floppy tails they thought they were half-fish and half-woman. They called them sirens, or mermaids.

Those sailors had great imaginations. They didn't seem to notice their "mermaids" were all bald with wrinkled faces and wiry whiskers. The sailors probably really saw manatees!

The skin of a manatee is mostly hairless but the whiskers on the snout are very sensitive.

Like the end of the elephant's trunk, manatee lips can work together to grasp and pull food into the manatee's mouth. Its flippers help hold the food.

Dugong
Steller's sea cow
Manatee

There are three types, or species (SPEE-sees), of manatees. All three are in danger of dying out, or becoming extinct. They are the Amazonian manatee, the West African manatee, and the West Indian manatee. They have many things in common and some differences.

Gliding through the water, all manatees look like small submarines. An average adult is about 10 feet (3 meters) long and weighs about 1,000 pounds (454 kilograms). Some may grow to 13 feet (4 meters) and weigh as much as 3,500 pounds (1,600 kilograms). Females are usually larger than males.

Manatees have thick, rough skin. They have a blimp-shaped body with two short, wide flippers and a flat, paddle-shaped tail. Their eyes are black and small, and widely spaced. They also have a broad snout with two nostrils, each about the size of a penny. Their brain is the size of a softball.

Both the West African and the West Indian manatee have three or four fingernails on each flipper. An Amazonian manatee does not have any fingernails.

West Indian and West African manatees are brown or light gray. The Amazonian is a much darker gray with white or pink patches on its belly.

The Amazonian lives only in freshwater lakes and rivers in the Amazon River area in South America. West African manatees are found along the western coast of Africa. They can live in fresh water, salt water, or a combination of the two, called brackish water. The West Indian manatee also can live in any type of water. It is the species people see in North America. Sometimes it is called the Florida manatee.

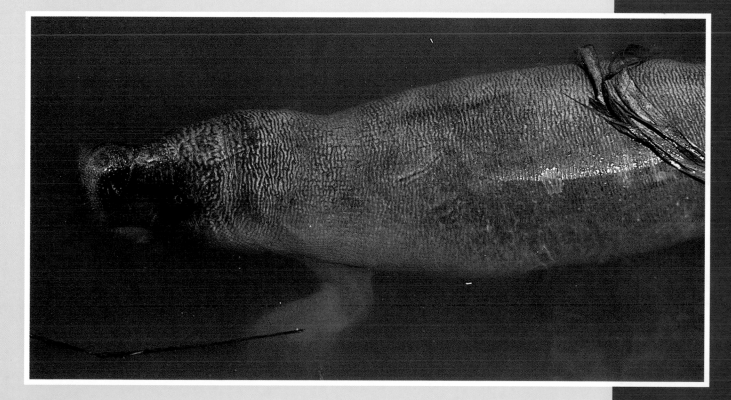

When the water where the Amazonian manatee lives is not very clear, it uses its flippers to help find food.

Manatees also have two relatives in the Sirenia order, the dugong and the now-extinct Steller's sea cow. Dugongs are smooth-skinned, dark-gray marine mammals with 10 to 14 teeth and a split, flipper-like tail. They are slimmer and shorter than the manatee, growing to only about half its size. Dugongs are found in warm waters of eastern Africa and northern Australia. They also live in Indonesia and the Phillippines.

Manatees and dugongs need warm water to survive. But Steller's sea cows thrived in cold water. They once lived in the icy arctic waters of the Bering Strait. Steller's sea cows were nearly three times larger than manatees. They were toothless, and also had a forked tail.

These dark brown creatures were named for George Wilhelm Steller, the German scientist who discovered them. They were hunted for their meat and blubber. And by 1768 they were extinct.

Dugongs rest in deep water during the day and move toward the shoreline at night to feed. They use their flippers for balance as they move along the ocean floor.

There is no real leader in a group of manatees. They all just seem to get along with each other.

Manatees are nomadic (no-MAD-ik), which means they wander. They have no permanent homes and they do not protect a specific area, or territory. They live in the warm, shallow water along the shore and cannot survive in cold water. These mammals require water temperatures of 68 degrees Fahrenheit (20 degrees Celsius) or above. They have a thin layer of fat called blubber underneath their skin. This blubber helps to keep the manatee warm.

When the winter weather turns the water colder, manatees migrate, or move, to where the water is warmer. Some manatees travel only a short distance to find nearby warmer water. But some travel hundreds of miles. Scientists think manatees return to the same warm-water sites each year.

During winter months, West Indian manatees are found in rivers, bays, springs, and canals in Florida. Some of them spend their Florida winters near electrical power plants. These factories are located near water sources. When special engines in power plants create electricity, cold water is used to cool them down. This creates warm water that is pumped out of the plant. This is where the manatees gather.

In the summer, West Indian manatees travel as far west as Louisiana and north along the East Coast to South Carolina, North Carolina, and Virginia. They have been spotted as far north as Rhode Island and as far south as Brazil in South America.

Manatees usually prefer water near shore from 5 to 20 feet (1.5 to 6 meters) deep. But they have been seen in very deep water as far as 4 miles (10 kilometers) offshore.

Manatees are always investigating new things that may
come into their habitat, including a school of fish.

When plants are plentiful in an area, manatees do not need to
travel very far to find food.

Manatees eat only plants, so they are called herbivores (HERB-uh-vorz). Their favorite foods include seagrasses, sea lettuce, and water hyacinths. They also eat mangrove leaves that fall into the water. The manatee's stomach contains a special bacteria that helps digest these tough, chewy plants. It takes nearly seven days for a manatee's digestive system to process one meal.

They can spend up to eight hours a day just eating. Manatees may eat up to sixty different kinds of aquatic, or water, plants. An adult manatee may eat more than 100 pounds (45 kilograms) of water plants each day. It needs to eat so much because these food sources are very low in energy-producing calories.

Every day manatees must search for food. They are farsighted and can see far away to distances of about 130 feet (40 meters). But like some humans who need glasses to read, manatees don't see well up close. They cannot rely only on their eyesight to find the right kind of food.

Manatees
FUNFACT:

Manatees usually don't dive more than 10 feet (3 meters). But they can dive as deep as 33 feet (10 meters), which is about the height of a three-story building.

Manatees have short, stiff whiskers on their lips and snouts. They work like sensors. When these sensitive hairs brush against plants, manatees usually find their next meal, even at night and in muddy water.

A manatee's upper lip is large and separated into two sections. A manatee can use them to grab plants with its mouth without turning its head. Manatee flippers have five "finger" bones, which are similar to bones in a human hand. They help the manatee grab plants by using the flippers like arms. Or it may use its flippers to pull itself halfway onto river banks. There, it feeds on land plants that grow near the water's edge.

Manatees do not have front teeth. They first chew their food using the short, sharp pads that line the inside of their lips. Then they grind the food with their big, flat back teeth, called molars. Manatees have between 24 and 32 molars on their upper and lower back jaws.

The sea vegetation that manatees eat is covered with sand, which eventually wears down their teeth as they chew. Those worn teeth fall out, and new ones push forward from the back of the mouth. Scientists call them "marching" teeth. And manatees can grow an endless supply of them.

After every meal, manatees clean their teeth. They remove the dirt and grasses caught between teeth by rolling small rocks around inside their mouths. Then they spit out the rocks!

Sometimes a manatee may use an anchor rope like dental floss to clean its teeth!

A manatee's tail must be very strong to move its large and heavy body through the water.

Manatees move through the water by pumping their powerful tails up and down. They navigate, or steer themselves, with their flippers. They also move on shallow river bottoms by using their flippers to pull themselves along.

Manatees
FUNFACT:

Manatees do not have eyelashes. They do have a transparent eyelid that slides across each eye. It works like goggles to protect the eyeball from salt water.

Manatees make good parents. This West Indian manatee mother is carefully showing her young where to find the best food.

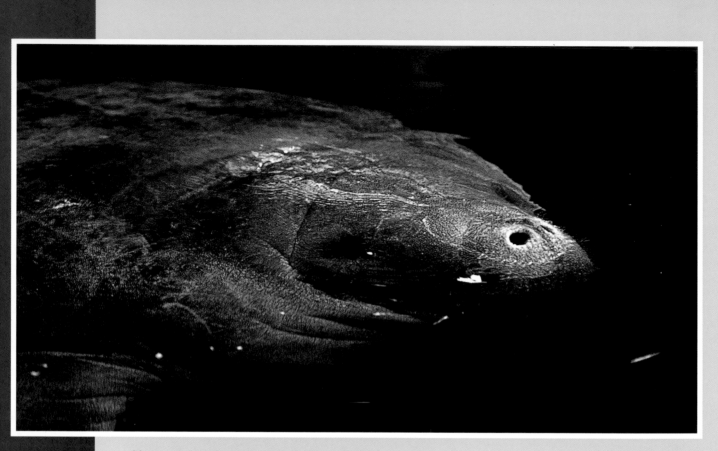

Manatees don't breathe through their mouths, just through their nostrils.

Manatees swim slowly and stop often to eat plants, which is called grazing. They travel at about 2 to 6 miles (3 to 10 kilometers) per hour. But if they need to move quickly, manatees can speed up to 15 miles (24 kilometers) per hour.

Because manatees usually swim so slowly, barnacles can attach themselves to their bodies. These underwater parasites, or freeloaders, may fasten onto manatees for free rides. Barnacles also can catch food from the water's currents as the manatee swims or rests on the bottom.

Manatees may also become covered with algae (AL-gee), which gives them a green or blue color. It makes them look like they have a skin disease, but it is not harmful.

Manatees get rid of this greenish plant slime by constantly shedding small pieces of skin. When their skin flakes off, the algae and barnacles also disappear.

Manatees can stay underwater for 15 to 20 minutes, but they usually surface to breathe air every 3 to 5 minutes They breathe by poking their nostrils into the air. They even float up for air in the middle of a snooze, then sink right back down to continue sleeping. Their nostrils have special flaps of skin that open when they surface and shut when they submerge (sub-MERJ), or go underwater.

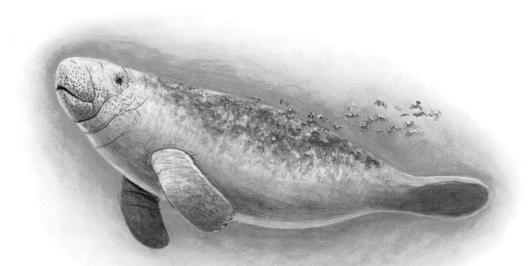

This sleeping manatee makes a good hiding place or shelter for a passing fish.

A normal day for a manatee is spent swimming, eating, resting, and playing. Manatees often sleep on their sides or upside down on their heads. They rest from 2 to 12 hours each day, floating near the surface of the water or on the bottom of a spring or river-bed. When resting or diving for food, a manatee's heartbeat slows to just once every 10 to 15 minutes.

Scientists who study animals are called zoologists (zoe-OL-uh-jists). They have learned that manatees exercise when they play. They bend, flex, and stretch. Manatees can balance in the water on their heads or on their tails. And they twirl through the water doing barrel rolls and somersaults. Sometimes manatees ride the water currents flowing down-stream. They look as if they are body surfing!

Manatees
FUNFACT:

Zoologists can tell how old a manatee is by counting the number of growth rings on its ear bones. Each ring equals one year. Manatees may live as long as 60 years.

A group of manatees is called a herd. It includes males and females of all ages. Herds usually have 5 to 25 members. But groups of more than 50 have been seen together. When mating is over or another migration begins, they each go their own way.

Manatees are tactile (TAK-tul), which means they like to touch things and each other. When they are together in a herd, they greet one another by pressing their snouts together or by touching tails.

Manatees swim together by holding onto each other with their flippers. They often chase members of their herd and give each other friendly bumps.

These manatees are not "kissing," but touching
to identify one another.

27

For most of the year, manatees lead quiet, solitary lives. Males, or bulls, migrate alone. Females, or cows, also travel alone or with their young at their sides.

They only socialize, or spend time together, during the mating season and when migrating groups gather in warm-water areas.

Sometimes several manatees form a single line that looks as if they are playing "follow-the-leader." They dip, dive, and swim together like graceful dancers, resurfacing for air all at the same time.

Besides touching, manatees communicate with each other by making vocalizations (vo-kul-ize-A-shuns), or sounds. They can be chirps, grunts, squeaks, squeals, and whistles. They often make groaning noises as they stretch. Each sound sends a different message.

Sometimes members of a herd just like being close together.

You can easily see that the nostril on this manatee's snout is closed while it is swimming underwater.

Manatee ears look like slits on the sides of their heads. They do not have earlobes, but manatees have large ear bones that give them good hearing.

Another way manatees communicate is by leaving scent (SENT), or odor.

Manatees rub their chins, flippers, and tails on logs and stones in the water. Other manatees understand these messages by rubbing their snouts over the scent markings. They have a good sense of smell.

Manatees
FUNFACT:

The manatee has been featured on postage stamps from around the world, including the U.S. And the state of Florida has a special manatee license plate. Money from the sale of this license plate pays for programs to help the manatee.

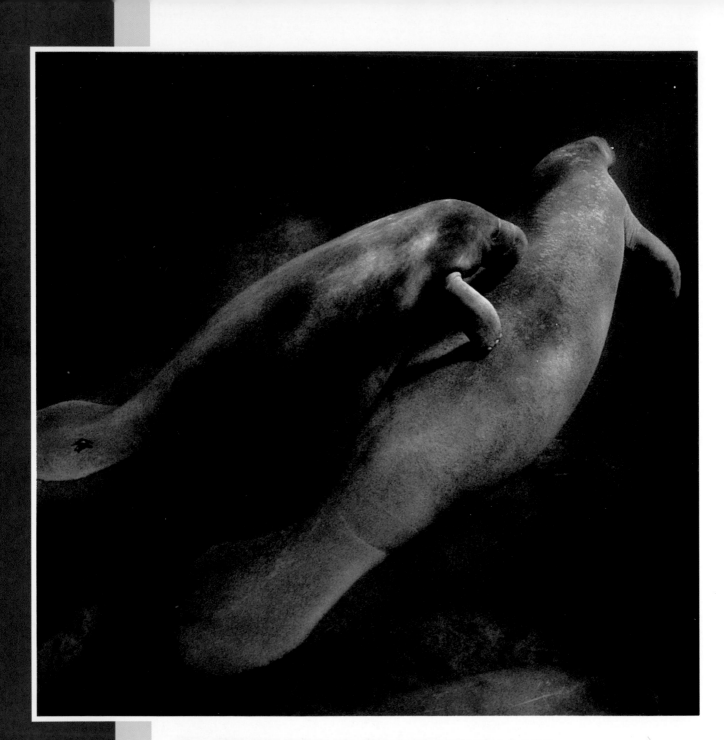

When manatees are ready to mate, the bull and cow stay close together, touching and rubbing each other with their flippers and bodies.

Females leave special scent messages when they are ready to mate. Cows are ready to mate at 5 to 9 years of age. Bulls are ready at about 9 years old. During the mating season, a cow and a bull nuzzle and hug each other.

Manatees do not mate for life. After mating, the male and female go their own way. Thirteen months later the cow gives birth and raises her baby alone.

Female manatees give birth every three to five years, mostly in spring and summer. They may have twins, but usually they have just one baby at a time. It may be born head-first or tail-first!

Manatees
FUNFACT:

Most mammals have seven neck bones, which allow them to turn their head sideways to see. Manatees have only six neck bones, so they must turn their whole bodies around to see.

A baby manatee is called a calf. After it is born underwater, the mother immediately pushes it above the surface for its first breath.

She then shows the calf how to go back down by pushing it underwater several times. The newborn already knows how to swim. As it grows, a calf has more blubber, which helps it float to the surface on its own.

A manatee calf is a tiny, dark-gray version of its mother. The calf turns a lighter gray or brown at about one month old.

A newborn manatee weighs at least 60 pounds (27 kilograms) and is about 4 feet long (1.2 meters). By the time it is one year old, it may weigh 700 pounds (315 kilograms) and be 6 feet (1.8 meters) long.

Mothers and calves often swim side by side,
and roll and play together.

Manatee mothers and their calves always stay close. And they constantly "talk" to each other in squeaks and whistles.

The calf nuzzles close to its mother's side even when it is not nursing. It sleeps snuggled underneath its mother's flippers, on her back, or even on her tail!

A manatee mother teaches her calf which plants to eat, how to migrate to warmer waters, and how to play. Sometimes it seems as if they are playing a game of tag.

But she also may swat her calf with her flippers. Or sit on her calf. Researchers say these are ways the mother teaches her youngster to behave.

This young calf is resting on its mother's tail. It's a good way to keep in contact with her.

If there is no seagrass nearby, a hungry young calf sometimes eats the algae that has grown on its mother's back.

It seems that calves are hungry all the time. They may nurse anytime during the day or night.

If a mother manatee finds her calf in danger, she puts her body between her young and the predator, or enemy, such as a shark or crocodile. But instead of fighting, the mother will try to escape by leading her calf away.

Like most mammals, a young manatee's first food is its mother's milk. A newborn quickly learns to nurse underwater.

When the calf is 2 or 3 months old, it begins tasting some seagrasses, but nursing continues for about 1 year. With both kinds of food, a calf gains up to 2 pounds (1 kilogram) each day during the first year.

When a manatee is 2 years old, it is ready to live on its own. But it's not unusual for offspring to remain in contact with their mothers. Sometimes they travel back to the place where their mothers live.

Manatees are friendly toward people. And they are naturally curious. When they find a human in the water, they often nudge the swimmer with their big snouts. Or they follow the human like huge dogs that want to be scratched or petted.

It may seem like great fun, but zoologists say this contact can be dangerous for the manatee. By connecting humans with kindness, manatees often get too close to people and their boats.

When boats speed through their habitats, manatees may be accidentally injured. In Florida, manatees are protected by laws that limit boat speeds. Special sanctuaries have been created to keep boats away from the manatee's habitat.

Even though manatees swim very slowly, they may sneak up on a boat and surprise the people.

Manatees often swim in pairs or groups. They like to stay in contact by touching each other.

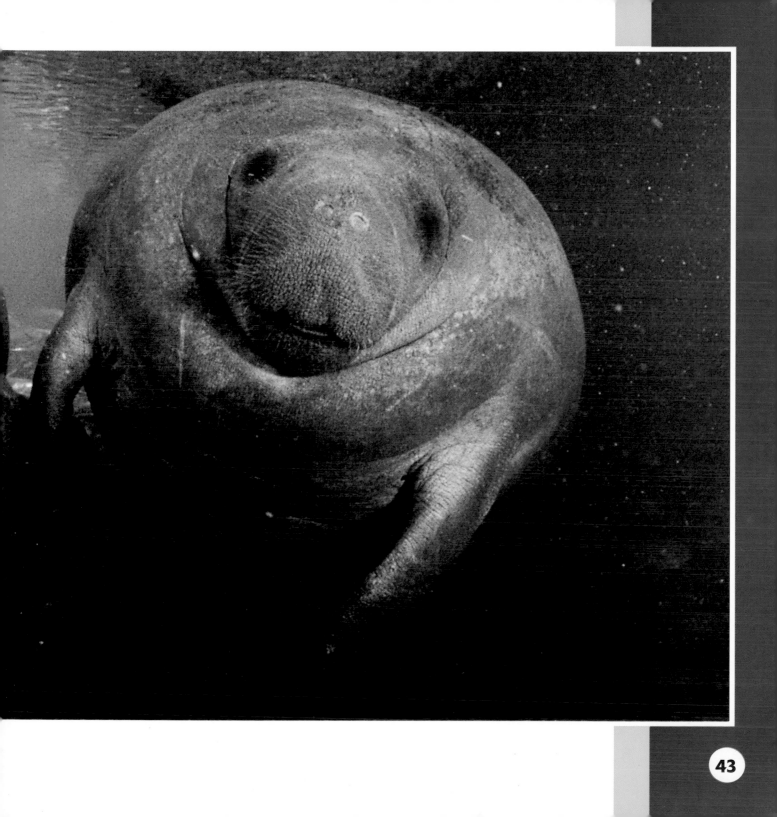

The peaceful manatee is easy to identify. It may not really be a mermaid, but it is beautiful in its own way.

Some manatees have been found tangled in fishing lines and crab traps. Others have died after swallowing fish hooks, fishing lines, or garbage such as plastic bags. Manatees lose their habitats when people pollute their waters or destroy their food sources.

Injured manatees are taken to rehabilitation centers to heal. Then they are returned to the wild.

One natural threat to manatees is a water bacteria called red tide. It turns the water red and can paralyze manatees and prevent them from surfacing for air.

Fortunately, manatees have many human friends. From school children to educational and scientific research groups, we are working together to protect manatees. With everyone's help, these "gentle giants" will continue to share our world.

Internet Sites

You can find out more interesting information about manatees and lots of other wildlife by visiting these Internet sites:

www.animal.discovery.com   Discovery Channel Online

www.enchantedlearning.com   Enchanted Learning.com

www.floridamarine.org   Florida Marine Research Institute

www.kidsplanet.org   Defenders of Wildlife

www.nwf.org   National Wildlife Federation

www.nationalgeographic.com/kids   National Geographic Society

www.savethemanatee.org   Save the Manatee Club

www.worldwildlife.org   World Wildlife Fund

Index

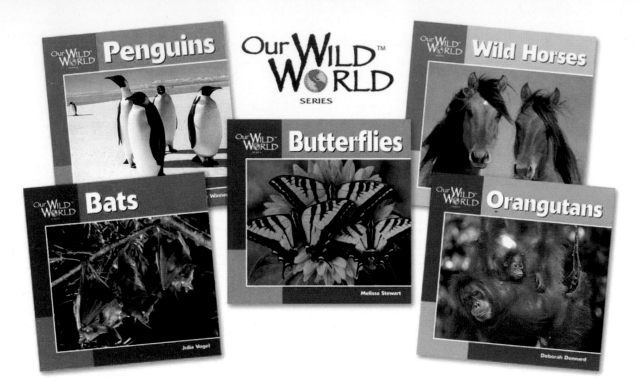

Titles available in the Our Wild World Series:

NorthWord
Minnetonka, Minnesota